Before I Lose Myself

By: LaVera Gene't

ISBN: 9781976776922

All Illustrations by: LaVera Gene't

Part 1: Heartbreak Conquered
Part 2 Letting Go Triumphed
Part 3: Love Won

Heartbreak Conquered

Long gone are the days that I rely on words and no action.
Or feel less than because of another human being.
-So long, farewell

Rebuilding oneself is a necessary in growth.
Healing is understanding one's soul.
-Growth

Realizing you've wasted time with a boy who had no intention of growing with you feels much like selling yourself for a dime bag of weed.

-Puff-Puff Pass

How is it that the sun beat you home?
How is it that when you came home from the gym your shirt was still crisply ironed, smelling of your cologne?
How is it that she could describe the details of our bedroom,
Yet she was the one that was lying?
How is it that all of a sudden the way that I take you all the way in,
Swallowing every drop, doesn't feel good anymore?
How is it that you've mastered how to make me cum by tongue kissing my clitoris? You were never that skilled before.
How is it that your face appears on dating websites and it is filled with recent activity?
How is it that your business trips included receipts of 2 meals, martini orders, room service of chocolate covered strawberries, and condom purchases?
How is it that you still deny ever having eyes for anyone else?
It was never your eyes that were the problem. You kept your dick busy.
-How

You left the same way you came: with 6 duffle bags and your heart intact.

-Nomad

One of these days you'll come to realize that he was never about you.
You were never sunshine in his eyes.
One of these days you'll stop crying over him.
-Oh Mister Sun.

I was told that men are the stronger than women.
When their bodies become the portal in which heaven meets earth to bring forth an entire human, let me know.
-Man, minus the womb

I don't think you're used to this struggle; the war to balance your needs with my own.
This becomes the line of where we differ.
-Seesaw

I fight for acknowledgement.
Got nothing in return
I yell, scream, cry angrily and still
You remain still- unable to bend
I say the right words to trigger your emotions
It is only then that you see me
It is only then that your posture changes
And your eyes stare piercingly at me
Do you see me now?
No. What you see is that you've been disrespected
That I-Tried-You
How dare I make you upset
The cycle...
Now you have fuel, ammunition
A valid reason to stay mad
A valid reason to tell me that we aren't growing
A valid reason to walk out the door
All of my pain dangles right in front of you
But you don't see it; all you see is
That I-Tried-You
The cycle...
So you make me feel less than
When all of this could have been avoided
If-You-Took-Time-To-Care-For-Me
The way I cared for you
I was once told that not everyone thinks like me
And to never take shit from anyone
True- but you...
It was supposed to be different.
-Mr. Tinman

One of the most selfish acts a man can do is tell you he wants to relieve your stress as he cums all over you.
-Nutty Business

How dare you plant seeds in her womb and leave before the harvest.
You're a coward.
I thought you should know.
-FYI

My younger self tried to warn me when she said: "Be careful of the boys who pretend to be men".
They'll rob you of your peace and have you wishing you were a little girl again.
-Thief

There's nothing humane about conquering land.
There's nothing humane about conquering people.
There's nothing humane about power or control.
To anyone that begs to differ:
You have no soul.
#

Tonight was the night I "took it too far".
Tonight was the night I heard confessions about how I was the cause of all of your stress.
Tonight was the night you proved me right; you were biding time.
Tonight was the night you broke up with me and almost broke me.
I almost drowned tonight.
-The last chapter

I despise you for wasting several fruitful years of my life.
I despise you for stringing me along because you knew I was a keeper.
I despise you for even putting forth the effort to bond with my daughter.
I despise you for breaking her heart.
I despise you for not being capable of showing her the way her beautiful mother deserves to be treated.
I despise you for leaving me to construct a decent explanation as to why you slept on the couch most nights, or weren't home when she woke up.
Fuck that, I hate you for that part.
All of this anger will turn into an abundance of thanks.
My daughter will see the polarity of a grown man vs one that has so much to learn.
-I'll forgive you, but not today.

1. Gather all of the photos of the memories you collected together and put them in a box. A pretty one, because healing from pain is a beautiful thing
2. Delete phone numbers. Block them from every outlet available to contacting you.
3. Delete every picture you ever took of you/the two of you.
4. Allow yourself to cry. This doesn't make you weak. Besides, these types of tears are good for your complexion.
5. Drink tea in the morning and self-reflect. My favorite is lavender and chamomile. The only way to heal from the pain is to dive in it.
6. Forgive yourself for thinking that it was ever okay to dim your light so that they could shine brighter. You were never meant to be in the background.
7. Treat yourself to a movie date. Find the latest showing, in the middle of the week, and bring one of your favorite blankets. When you get inside, walk up to the middle of the theatre and pick the seat that feels right. There may be 3 or 4 people in the whole theatre but it'll still feel like the movie is playing in the middle of the week, just for you. You deserve that.
8 .As hard as it might be, make sure you eat. Your body has yet to give up on you. A lover deprived you of enough already; nourish your body.
9. Place your hand on your chest, breath calmly and deep and feel the beat of your heart. Remind yourself that this isn't the end of your world. Repeat this as many times as it takes for you believe it. You will recover from this.
10. Buy all new panties and bed sheets. Energy has a way of lingering in fabric.
11. Put a few check marks on that bucket list of yours.
12. Live freely, continue to love deeply. That is what makes you so damn magical.
-Before the glow up
(An ode to Rupi Kaur)

You've become a puzzle piece to my life's journey that I foolishly lost and am still searching for. I tried to find it in the stores, online, everywhere but no luck. Because the thing about this puzzle piece is that it's a classic; much like true hip hop. All others are just failed revisions of the original. Foolish girl I was. Foolish woman I became.
-Dear Mr. Hip Hop

Love should always be turned into poetry.
Especially the ones that make your heart break in two
-Poetry

It's okay not to be okay.
It's okay to seek comfort in the ones that love you the most.
It's okay to laugh until you cry, realizing it is the pain that is seeping through. Let your soul rain when needed.
It's okay to admit that you need help recovering.
It's okay to be soft.
-It's okay

Letting Go Triumphed

The quickest way to lose your love is to show them just how much you don't care.
Actions will forever be the first language.
-Your loss

Only allow your significant other to tell you 'I'm not ready, I need more time' no more than once.
If you make it to two you'll soon realize...all they're doing is biding time while wasting yours.
-Assets & Liabilities

Everything about you has become so pathetic to me.
Your ego is so big but the man in you is so small.
You place your debonair mask on; making sure you're ready to fool the world for another day.
A role you play quite well.
It is now my current fascination.
I'm mystified that someone so selfish and broken can pretend to be brand new.
You should've taken your mask off before you washed your ass.
It's starting to rust.
Thespian

You weren't my first choice but I chose you first
I should have let you stay in your own lane; you were never my speed
But I wanted you to be
-Confession

The moment when you realize that it's no longer "we".
But simply you, then me.
-Final Hour

Shame on me for living a watered down version of myself in order for you to feel top shelf.
-Dry, no ice

One: I'm finally done
Two: The joke's on you
Three: I never came when you fucked me
Four: My Yoni was never yours
Five: Your entire being is the only thing I despise
-I learned to lie from you

Why do we continue to let the black men we love so much break us? Perhaps the years of watching them be emasculated is codified in the memory of our DNA.

Perhaps we soak up the pain with the hope that this will be the cycle, the lifetime that they finally gain their power back. The price for that is, losing ours.

-Perhaps

I prefer the version of you that was sold to me originally. More than what is in front of me

I'd like my refund please.

- Salesman

Dear ex-lover: Pride and immaturity will have you thinking the wrong people are your enemies.
Learn to conquer your former self.
-Maturity Malfunction

I forgive myself for going back.
I forgive myself for fighting him
I forgive myself for losing my desire to desire him
I forgive myself for wanting more progress from him, because in the end he was not the one to build with
I forgive myself for not being patient enough, and tired of waiting on someone else to feel comfortable
I forgive myself for hating this outcome much more than I loved the person it was created with.
-When you fall in love with potential

Today is going to be beautiful.
That was the declaration I made before my feet even hit the floor.
Today is going to be beautiful.
I completely prayed and saged you out of my existence.
It must've worked because it's been months since you came around.
Today will be beautiful.
My work for the day awaits and the last two scoops of my favorite tea are brewing.
Today will be beautiful.
The fan is on, I finished my tea, but it's so hot in here.
Today will still be beautiful.
It's too hot in here. It's becoming harder to breathe now.
This isn't the day I had in mind; this is hell at the moment.
Today will still be OK.
You're here. Rising from within.
Determined to stomp all over my progress.
I feel you crawling up my arm. I hate having to shake it in this weird way.
You enjoy making a fool of me.
You won't get me.
Today will still be OK.
See, it's so much cooler in here now. And my arm is back to normal.
I told you today will be OK.
Everyone is annoying me. They want nothing but love but I can't seem to give it.
Fuck…Fuck you and this day.
You're the type that makes me look like I'm in a fit of rage in front of other people, even in front of myself.
Who am I? I don't even recognize this reflection. My eyes look dilated.
FUCK. THIS. DAY.
You go for my ears. Make them ring.
Ring so loud that I can't even hear the sound of my own soul desperately trying to find me, just to tell me to try and calm down.
Maybe if I go in my closet, sit on the floor with my knees to my chest you'll stop.
You don't stop.
You're making me hate this day.
The day I was determined to make beautiful.

The day I declared and manifested to be beautiful.

Time for your grand finale.

You make me cry.

It's different when you make cry because I don't even know why.

I don't know what part of this day would make me hyperventilate.

I don't know what part of this day would make me lose my thoughts. My senses.

Today was your day.

Dear Anxiety,

FUCK. YOU.

I'm sorry to my mind:
For trying to sway its calculated decisions
I'm sorry to my body:
For not being pleased with its appearance at times
I'm sorry to my soul:
For seeking refuge in the confines of disharmonious souls.
All I ever needed was me.
-I apologize

Loving me meant nurturing my health.
There came a point where eating dead animals no longer made me feel alive.
-Ex-Flesh eating addict

Did all of this soul searching, growing and developing new ways to move through life.

Not once did it occur to me to ask:

Are you even marriage material?

-Wasted

People will push you away and say that you gave up on them.
Go figure.

I allowed myself to feel the pain.
It is the greatest most precious gift I ever gave myself.
-Om

I used to think something was wrong with me because I let go of sadness sooner than others.
I'll cry, yes. Grieve even.
But it lasts about as long as my menses.
Maybe it is because subconsciously I was already preparing for my exit but my heart wouldn't let me move.
The end result is that I stay in relationships well past its expiration date.
-The gift. The curse

I'd prefer if you didn't occupy this space in my heart anymore
I know I asked for you a few years ago
But loving me is enough
Maybe I was asking for too much and for that I'm sorry
I promise I won't cry about it anymore
I know, I know…I know I said I wanted children
It's not that I don't anymore; I'm just coming to terms that it may not
happen when I want it to
Love, I love you I do
But when I've called on you, begged for you all I got was a watered down
version of you
There are no hard feelings
Really, there's not
Maybe instead of me asking for you
You could return the favor and search for me too.
-Dear love

Social media constantly exposes you to other people's deceptive realities;
Giving you glimpses of something you desire
It just isn't your time yet beloved.
There are so many layers to you and you've only peeled back a handful.
Let this be the last time you drag the future into your present.
-Just be

Who made you feel so inadequate that you would seek vengeance the moment
you feel wronged?
Can you feel how close you are to shattering?
Do you realize that if I try to catch you I will crumble in the process?
-The childhood wounds we carry

Do you know how freeing it is to answer a simple "how are you"
truthfully?
I'm spiritually and mentally healing, thanks for asking.
-Bandaged

You gave me a reason to let my guard down.
You also gave me a reason to put it back up.
-Dear J.

The outer appearance is as it should be: perfection.
But the inner, what is inside the home, the mind, is clutter.
Disorder.
A bunch of good intentions just lying around, waiting to be put to use
But never is. Because it is just an intention
You're the type that could ever meet me halfway.
-Broken finish line

There's too many women out here breastfeeding these man babies.
-Weaning season

You had the sun.
Basked in it at your disposal and it still wasn't enough.
If light can't make you want to do better, baby I don't know what will.
-Sun bath

Remaining stagnant in a relationship is not a sign from the universe saying you cannot go any further.
Learn to tune in to your intuition and not the empty promises and lies you were fed.
Or you'll always remain hungry.
-Malnourished

I am exactly where I need to be.
Which is far away from you-
Don't come for me.
-Go away

Don't you ever take my softness and vulnerability with you as me being weak.
I will still chew you up and spit you out.
-Now you know

Little boy blue
Let's take a look at you
Pretended to be a man to get a woman to notice you.
Now you have her hooked, her expectations got you shook
So you run and hide when she comes looking for you.
Little boy blue
You thought you would be fine
Dealing with a woman who always spoke her mind
There's no way you'll survive, she peeps game and knows your lies
Now you fear that everyone will notice you're in disguise.
Little boy blue
She's finally over you.
Now take off your grown man clothes
You have work to do.
-Little Boy Blue

Love Won

Sometimes my honesty is too aggressive. I know not how to express myself subtly, I've tried. It makes me unsettled and feeling like I must speak urgently; it's just not in me. Everything I speak and feel has depth.
-Go deep with me

Forever is never enough with you. Today, tomorrow and through our next lifetime...I Do.
-Dearly beloved

You have the blood of many warriors coursing through your veins.
I see the king in you.
Better yet, I feel it too.
-Dear King

I refuse to put black men down.
Especially when I am raising one.
-For my sun

Love ...isn't always glamorous. But when it's real, it's worth experiencing fully; mind, body and soul.

Nothing exists without its opposite. The universe designed it to be that way.

Sometimes if we laugh hard enough, we cry.

Sometimes when we cry reminiscent of a memory, we end up laughing at the end.

Wanting the best for a person even when they don't want it for themselves, still doing for a person when they've upset you, being genuinely happy for a person's growth without envy or jealousy...All of these things is love.

It's perfect. Thank you for helping me grow. Whether you realize it or not, you have

-New eyes

Kiss me as if your last breath depended on it.
-First Kiss

There's nothing wrong with vulnerability.

There's nothing wrong with giving your all, regardless of what the outcome.

There's beauty in the warrior that chooses not to bear arms in front of the ones they love.

When it is all said and done, you gave your all.

You gave your heart.

You gave your best.

The spirit that doesn't see the God in you doesn't deserve you.

-Lessons at 30

I have no fear of losing you, for you aren't my property, or anyone else's.
I love you as you are,
Without attachment,
Without fears,
Without conditions,
Without egoism.
Trying not to absorb you.
I love you freely because I love your freedom, as well as mine.
-No fear

Cheers to:
Putting myself first
Cheers to:
Falling in love with every part of me
Cheers to:
Healing my entire being
Cheers to:
Allowing myself the space to fall and stand up gracefully
-A toast

You've always been enough.
No more looking for nourishment that leaves you feeling empty.
You are just what the doctor ordered.
-Sasa
(For my sister and soul sistahs)

I have my father's eyes and my mother's cheekbones.
Through me they'll always be together.
-Cookie & Junie made me

I decided to wine and dine myself tonight and make love to the sweetest parts of me.
I thought it would be a solo performance until you crept in the crevices of my thoughts.
Your scent pierced the very air that I breathed as I climaxed.
Tonight I made love for two.
In my mind, there's always you.
-Solo performance

Love me hard.
Love me well.
And see how beautifully I soften.

Healing is not all about experiencing constant waves of happiness.
Feed the pain.
Feel the anger
And this, my dear, is how you grow.
-Heal

You gotta pray.
You gotta meditate.
You gotta eat well.
You gotta drink water.
You gotta get in the routine of maintaining good mental health.
-You just gotta

Emotions once tangled turned into a stream of poetry.
How freeing it is to heal this way.

There were transitions of absolute certainty:
I was fully aware of what I needed to do in order to create new patterns.
Then there's my recent transition:
Where I thought the path I was sailing on was OK because it was safe.
It took countless hours of meditation and my ancestors to intervene for me to realize how suffocated and overwhelmed I was.
All I could do was shut off and tune in.
Give me the attention and love I needed.
Finally.
I'm synching with the universe.
Finally.
I'm creating my own wave.
Finally.
I'm finding my way.

CPSIA information can be obtained
at www.ICGtesting.com
Printed in the USA
LVHW081558070119
603014LV00020B/671/P